(　　)

# Away From Me

*Caleb Klaces*

Caleb Klaces is the author of the novel *Fatherhood*
and the poetry collection *Bottled Air*.


Many of these poems arrive here having developed through
conversation, collaboration and prior publication:

'Sunrise' and 'Sunset' in *Poetry Review*

'Modern Version' as a pamphlet by If a Leaf Falls Press

'Duck's Poem About Rabbit' and 'Prisoner's Dilemma'
in *Blackbox Manifold*

'First Time Again' in *Poetry, The White Review* and
*The Best British Poetry 2015*

'Arguments for a Wall' in *Poetry London*

'IKT-SVO' by *Lunar Poetry Podcasts*

'Today' with Endre Ruset

'Love in reverse is evolution' with Daisy Hildyard,
prompted by Studio Swine, and advised by Jo Elworthy
at The Eden Project, in *NOON*

'world around the' in *The North* and by
New York Public Libraries

'Flying over "Mont Blanc"' in *WASTE*


I am grateful to everyone involved.
Thanks also to Oli, Magnus and Jess.

# Contents

| | |
|---|---|
| Sunrise | 14 |
| Modern Version | 18 |
| Middlemarch | 28 |
| Duck's Poem About Rabbit | 32 |
| Tuesday Night At The Grosvenor Hotel The Legendary Steve Phillips Plays The Blues: An Anecdote | 34 |
| | |
| First Time Again | 42 |
| | |
| Self-Rated AAA | 56 |
| The Price of Nuts | 58 |
| Arguments for a Wall | 62 |
| Today | 66 |
| | |
| Admin | 74 |
| | |
| The caged lion asks what being a father is like | 84 |
| Sequel | 92 |
| IKT-SVO | 94 |
| Prisoner's Dilemma | 98 |
| Satire | 102 |
| | |
| explanatory notes with no fingers | 110 |
| | |
| Love in reverse is evolution | 118 |
| world around the | 124 |
| The sun looks in and the whole world with it | 126 |
| Sunset | 128 |
| | |
| Flying Over 'Mont Blanc' | 136 |

# Sunrise

I turned the corner and spied a nice car.
I opened the door, pulled out the driver
and got in. I played music on the radio.
I drove along the road. It was dark and
the lights were broken. I screamed
around the corner and knocked another
car into a lamppost. I swapped vehicle
for a parked van. In the van the radio
made me feel odd. I drove through a
park. It was as though it was played on
the wrong instruments. It was empty
and confusing. It might just have been
another park. The driver from before
was running around the dark lake. I
turned off the radio. I drove around
the dark lake. I was driving around the
lake but then I headed for the power
station. The horizon in the window
was further than I thought. I drove
for a while. I felt odd with no music.
I parked the van. I found a pair of
headphones on someone else so that
I could listen to music while I looked
around the power station. I walked
along the pavement to the far corner.
I walked around the corner. Each of
the corners led to another one. I turned
in the other direction. It was the same.
But the original direction was better.
I span in that direction and took the

corners when they arrived. The sun
was coming up. There was a nice car
but I did not get it. I thought that around
the corner I would see something else.
There was sunlight coming through.
The headphones were gone. I threw
aside a manhole cover and climbed
down. In the tunnel water dripped
on water. There was so much light.
I walked through the tunnel. I walked
through the tunnel. I walked and then
it was too bright and then I went on.

# Modern Version

Years ago Gary tackled a mugger,
married the woman he saved
and started a private security firm.
Now June, a family friend,
is on her way to the converted
country estate where Gary's cadets
are trained before
tours abroad. Gary wants June
to oversee a disciplinary investigation.
The swimming pool, his secretary interjects,
was so bloody it had to be drained.
We are reassured this
is the beginning:
there has been a fight in the swimming pool
between Portia, a woman who is an instructor,
and an unnamed male cadet
she was instructing.
June hears
Portia does not have a violent past,
no one has been particularly violent towards her.
It is the historical violence against women
makes her angry.
June says Portia would look so much more
sensible with some make-up.
Around the base we see men
shovelling human waste
('shit').
They sing a song
interpreted as
about a woman eating them.

This is the first connection between
music and violence, violence against women
and women who are violent.
Gary does indeed make June
feel secure and protected
as he explains over dinner his company's role
is never aggressive.
We are introduced to Jake,
Gary's son, who works
at the firm and is ready to become chief executive
when his father retires in a few months.
Portia, we learn, 'eats'.
Her relationship is with the person
responsible for food on the base.
Ian is short. On our first meeting with him
he and Jake are overly friendly outside the office,
obviously don't like one another.
Jake is negotiating a contract with Ian
for taking away human waste
('regret') from the base and in return
supplying the base with energy.
The fields once grew corn
and Ian supplies food
while Portia will not eat it.
Yet they are in love.
Everyone on the base
is making energy from food without even
thinking about it, except Portia
who is thinking about it.
Portia has tremendous power over

the men in particular of the base,
whose disgust and desire are connected.
The description of her power is intense.
The men can't believe she
has tricked them into...
Her fight in the swimming pool
reveals to the men
they will be overrun.
The man she attacked in the swimming pool
has lost a finger. He is happy about it.
He tells June surely they cannot
fire him now he has given them
his finger.
Ian dies suddenly. There is some plot.
Portia, described
as angry, is with June
when Ian dies
so she is where
she is where
she is where
she is where
she is where...
Typically, this concludes with a discussion
of a female saint who lived on nothing
but communion wafer and who
had visions and cured infected men.
Jake screams at a woman
walking her dog on the perimeter.
In her anger and grief, Portia sleeps
with Jake. June is jealous

though she does not want to sleep with Portia or Jake.
She imagines Jake's sticky ejaculation.
Portia sounds like portion and apparition.
Jake had planned to humiliate and impress his father
by showing the deal with Ian for the base's waste,
which Gary desperately wanted for his base
('elsewhere') and also
for his conscience,
was corrupt because Ian was corrupt.
But Ian died. The following
becomes a mystery about the death
of Ian because how and why did he die?
Why do people die?
There are two other main characters.
Hana-Sue is second in command to Gary.
She is always described,
when after some searching
we finally locate her in a room, as having little
or no body to speak of,
not at all like Portia, who starves her body,
but rather in a metaphorical way,
with Hana-Sue seeming to be elsewhere
even when we come upon her.
('She talked about something else.')
She has twin male children
who, kissing one another,
weigh down the room with male body.
Hana-Sue also dreams of becoming the chief executive.
Would she have killed Ian?
Ian knew of her affair with the janitor

but what difference does that really make to Hana-Sue?
Jake could have killed Ian because he was in love with Portia.
There is no reason for Gary to kill Ian.
Gary sings a single Karaoke
at the 'tavern' on Saturday night
which employees and cadets must attend.
The theme of violent music.
It is at one such Karaoke that
events come to a head. Gary's wife,
Jake's mother, is drunk.
Wow, she shouts!
Jake and Gary almost come to blows
over a description of Portia
('sapling' or 'firewood') and Gary swears
in a moment long recognised for its great beauty
he will crown Hana-Sue chief executive
of his security firm.
Meanwhile we have learnt much about
the families of the characters.
What we have learnt about the families
is also about food, globalisation, giving,
withholding and the subjugation of women.
At the same time Portia's sole ally,
the only man not under her spell,
which is ironic,
has embarked on a hunger strike
in protest at her investigation following
the fight in the swimming pool.
Blood.
His hunger strike is earnest and Portia

appreciates the gesture but
along with us and the other characters
is confused and embarrassed.
Luckily for Portia
by this point there is a flood.
Gary assembles the cadets
and orders them into the village
to assist local people.
'Animals' rise
to the surface.
This is easily the first true climax
because of our togetherness and purpose.
Portia and Gary
lead everyone through the dirty water.
June keeps asking Gary
where his wife is. This is compared
to 'the blocked drain'.
We learn the weight of the water
the janitor drained from the pool.
The janitor is a deliberately poor
character, either a wise fool or a Christian
who forced Hana-Sue to bear a child
rather than abort it.
June's husband studied music because
it lifted him out of his teenage body.
There is also a passage in which he describes
to a distracted June
becoming a father.
His wife recovered well
but he the father became badly constipated.

('The man lost his voice.')
The water subsides.
There is another warm night of Karaoke.
Jake and Hana-Sue accuse Gary
of murdering Ian to distract
attention from what he has accused them
of. 'Roxanne' fades out,
Gary orders Ian's body be brought
by the janitor, who has been storing it
in the old ice house, so that Gary may
perform an autopsy 'now'.
Gary assumes
he can do what he likes
with another body
because he tackled a mugger
and is chief executive of a private security firm.
('Giorgio Agamben.')
Spectators are sobering up.
The body is duly wheeled in by the janitor
who we spy then in a corner
embraced by Hana-Sue, who
to our great relief is described in her body.
Gary takes a penknife and slits Ian's dead stomach.
At that moment Portia enters.
Gary has indeed found a golden key
inside Ian's guts
like a key to the story.
Did Ian anticipate this?
There is a moment when
Gary, who is holding the key,

looks as though he would fight
to the death anyone who attempted to take
the body away from him.
Jake shows unexpected courage to tell his father:
Father, let Portia have the body which is hers.
Sure enough she walks over, picks up
a fistful of Ian's guts and eats them.
This makes sense.
Have something to eat, Portia.
The man on hunger strike is sent to hospital.
Jake inherits the business and it becomes
more financially successful.
June reports that Portia was
attacked in the swimming pool
and Jake promotes Portia.
June swims in the pool on the base.
She hears imaginary music while she swims.
On her last day she goes there
and has the man who lost his finger
on her conscience. A male cadet brushes past
June in the pool
and she attacks.
The janitor lumbers in
to drain the pool again.
Portia achieves her wish to be sent on what
they call a tour of duty
and is killed by a bomb.
Ian's body is collected by his mother,
a very quiet, dignified,
private and accepting woman,

the government's top adviser
on nutrition,
who believes whatever happened to her son's body
is his business.

# Middlemarch

Amir kneels to watch a shoal pass through another shoal.

Jamila asks her companions the name of the waiter.

Freya plays 'Brothers in Arms' with her band Around the Wall.

Fish nibble rice in Hari's dishwater.

Karl stops his tram for a samba band.

Neil glances at the wing mirror and then at his phone.

Caleb hurries through the uneven scrubland.

Oraib convinces the family not to return home.

Basak mops up sauce from her mother's plate.

At the orphanage Xavier greets the new children.

Dusan looks in the box to find a good net.

Once settled on the train Qiu eats a steamed bun.

Rael's friend is upset and Rael holds his friend's hand.

Seunghwan sings and rolls over in her sleep.

Gabriel spends some time checking on the odd sound.

Mingmar looks for caterpillar fungus on the slope.

Thea chews along with the music.

Valerie sucks a mint with her eyes on the stars.

Pierre hops towards his other sock.

Udu rubs his big toe while he says his prayers.

Ivan opens the plug of his sewing machine.

Yesenia tucks a stranger into her own bed.

Eray starts the car and leaves it running.

Wasilei laughs because his leg has gone dead.

Lara enters the stage and unbuttons her gown.
Zhanna giggles while she pretends to frown.

# Duck's Poem About Rabbit

The doctor didn't ask why I wanted to leave. When I was young we were very little. Leaves should never be that colour. Nobody glistens. My sister whistled back. Every photograph I look less like the photographs. The hospital's most significant inefficiency was Robert Walser. They won't be smiling when I get my heritage. Million billion trillion billion million. When I was young I had to be a boy. It tastes different. Someone shouted at me. I was murdered. I was ground up and passed off as horse. My sister was kept to a minimum. The way arrogant owners let their best friends, Robert Walser lay down and they could drink the melted snow. I just take out my aids. It's enough of a joke. They'd grow me again if I went the Zurich route. The world won't fit. Soiled fingers all over the fields. You won't make sense of the wiring. The corner fails to beat the first man. (No discipline.) I love the hat but I hate them for making me wear it. One word for my line manager is shrill. He eats through a straw and takes the Robert Walser out of the nurses. When he clipped my Achilles with his trolley his baby laughed. I was taught to be polite. It feels like the part that's bacteria. It feels like losing.

# Tuesday Night At The Grosvenor Hotel The Legendary Steve Phillips Plays The Blues: An Anecdote

*NACHOS topped with tomato salsa and chesse*
    *sauce with guacomole and sour cream dips*
so enormous already expanded yet further
    with a blue warmth into my walls like

the cavities men speak of in the locker room.
    *You have cared too much how to spell cheese,*
said the thick green notes and said the sad, spicy words.
    My objective was to get to weep,

which Steve Phillips claimed he himself was doing,
    although he looked basically content,
on the banks of the Owichita. Could I point
    to Louisiana on a map? My phone undresses

itself at my fingertip. I mean it, this isn't—
    I'm not trying to catch you out. Or me
out. I really did lay my burden down at the
    feet of Steve Phillips and really did

recall that Yorkshire people owned slaves.
    Henry Lascelles, 2nd Earl of Harewood,
for example, owner of 1,277, Thursday night
    at the City of London Tavern, 1832, declared,

'I, among others, am a sufferer,' indicating
    the distress those respectable men
and women proprietors laboured under.
    What would become of the men, women

and children of the English Midlands
        who forged the locks and the chains?
The suffering in the blues that fills
        Steve Phillips on a Tuesday at the Grosvenor

Hotel is the suffering which built the Grosvenor
        Hotel. I listened to the suffering
and I heard my own suffering. I was like:
        'I wish Dad could say something nice

about my poems.' I was like: 'Why are adults
        so frightened when I plait my
daughter's hair?' Steve Phillips drew close
        his microphone and the copper

miners' houses fell into the hole where
        copper had been. Steve Phillips, my ears
told me, had suffered so much, whipped
        on the banks of the Mississippi—

no, that's not right! I had planned this whole
        bit where Steve Phillips gives voice
to the time he worked in a smartphone
        factory. Steve's job was to inspect

each lens for a scratch. I was dreaming

        his blues, like: 'I woke up this morning,
to work for Foxconn,' a simple list of the names

given by factory colleagues to babies
who had died. Then I thought: 'If that's the song

you want to write then you should write that song.'

# First Time Again

across an empty sea. Rising from my lounger

I could not remember whether I had my dong on.
Round the saltwater pool undergraduates Yes to sexy
No to desperate. I had picked up their way with vowels
and was making up for it with inimitable consonants.
What I saw leave the hollow of my open hand, wobble
as if played from a speaker through palm trees' blue
shade several windows deep was what a lepidopterist
would recognise as an image in lieu of a real moth.


Bodies have no such exchange Balloons to include me
inside it, from across the water. Spray from each dive

sharpens skin to a point. Pop. The frame Between his
thighs, moths span on their splintered golden wings
while the hot mind caught Plastic acquires a pet name.
Waking reported war, church bells on Audio inaudible
at ear height. All my blood in a pile. Reconnected me
with Cherry from English and a used phrase, 'the number
of things it is possible to think all at once.' The price of

The translation has more moths than the original.
Where clothes end, in lieu of the people themselves
People themselves. Each of us strains to be more

like the others than the others. Stealth's
angles make an obvious plane. One wants to find out
why the lover is not located in the body of the lover.
On a long wooden pier keen automatic men looked
to the ends of their lines six nights of the summer week.
They sensed extension in all directions but knew only


the difficulty of extension. More afraid of meaning
more than I mean I stay awake through the fun.
Casting off rain, the Wake from the agreement
to find one another by accident. Drawn from

suggestions the environment made, his large wet kisses,
whether I wanted to be included in her large wet kisses.
The bacterium alive on damp leaves of *The Game* lends
substance to the dimension I could not get hold of
between the gym and the gym on the gym TV.

See. Buried by clean linen. Sex is the pea. We have sex
on top of Our voices mean more than we mean.
Moth-phobic translator does a book with a moth motif,
spends three years with the question Those fuckers: do we
want to be them or to have them? The object of desire,

whether clothed as teacup or cherub, is also an objection.
A splinter in the leaves. Sunbathing woman becomes aware
of a hair clot shuddering between pimpled white slats
of an overspill slurp and sets and dives to feel the shaved


Fruit sells. It keeps summer inside, like a forecast
App for 'the number of things it is possible to think
all at once' decorates the urge, catching up with
To go at it quickly and hard, a sex-within-sex,
flight which is also reeling in. The water stung
her nose. A tent collapsed with us enormous inside

The pregnant woman shows us where in us
A replacement cherry skin. I can't tell you how
much of what I know is the inability to turn into

You, splintered like the one true cross in the body
of the hedgehog, for whom we put out milk and
Tyres shredded. Whether your moths are more real
or more cultured, I remember dry wings on water
inflating and popped by an Ext. Daytime. Wet
skin soliciting sun. The original author who was
merely fascinated. The late, great European poets

and a chalk outline where No punch-line here. Say it
With American genitalia, I knew desire setting


in the shape of a gelatinous missile. Blindly erect,
a blunt growl, a perfectly squeaking door. Requiring
sex once more to set sex right. And this while it
happened. Everything's parts everywhere To spread
globally Copy text with own emotion. Cherry pumped
my fingers with gas. Information does not resist fantasies
of weapons inspectors but affords them cool air
abundantly in the desert. Another, poorer, nation

loaded with images the shaft where experience collapsed.

Then it seemed suddenly possible to divide time into moments, or,
in fact, more accurately, for thinking to be so divided; an awareness,
then, I should say, that immediately following the present focus of attention,
which itself was, by virtue of that attention, smudged, resulting
in a discernible slowing and the creation, therefore, of space around
the present moment, where the attention placed on it exceeded
what it could be attentive to, so the present moment began to slip away

— we were translating 'passionate' into the original text.
She said she cleaned her teeth and cleaned her teeth —


before the anticipated moment had arrived, so a third moment,
brought into being by attention itself — as if it was censorship.
A folder A fig leaf placed over the photograph of the enemy
naked on the desktop. A window appears and through it Better.
So-called iceberg properties. If only the petals glued back on.
The water closed. The knickers climbed for the hand to disturb

for a first time. I sprinkled coins into the open coffin
as if they were money. White slats, slurping overspill, gold
sliding down the face. The instinct hooked in the mouth

in which Adam's mouth spoke, against 'death', without
quotation marks, in my mouth furious with thanks.
I meant to say the one great question is To whom or what
should I give my thanks? They automatically undress again.
Parts which sin grow plastic and large, more real and yet further

Balloon trapped in a moth's heart. Each eager stroke reduces
likelihood of sky, straining to extend below the waterline.
We are not one another. With that prefatory statement each,
they came. A dense blob of paint thinned with clear water.


Pale streaks Home to species invisible to the Passion pulled
away from me like an artificial fly. After he had been done
he noticed her steadying hand on the rubber travels ever so
slightly quicker than the escalator itself. View completed

by a competing view, even as the sum of the two views wants
completion, even as many affluent homes acquire new rooms
beneath to stay on top of Dragged the water into me. Instead,
the city shouts up to the bedroom window, 'We can't hear you.
We really have no idea what you are doing up there together.'

Foundation had collected in the throat, too shy to bring it up.
For that gift of extension into someone else was received
without growth or erosion. When asked if she was sexy

or desperate it appeared that she had no place in language.
Afterwards the objection became the lover. To undress,
to sleep with, in lieu of the People themselves are never
enough. Or too much. The pool itself drains me. Balloons
become cushions, the source becomes pale streaks of blue
Dribble. So many thoughts become one thought, and rather than


a thought they divided themselves into, it was a thought
divided by them. Catching You has the outside

arranged so that its inside is the landscape behind
the portrait. To replace childhood's broken chintz,
0.1% APR. For the price of light, a moth. State
the word to bring about agreement to use the word.
Sex is performed to make sex possible. Bodies rise
to meet bodies. Each line cast into the night sea
straightened with the same imagined flight. Each took in

the same weightless attention and offered the same slack.

Having closed in on death, the men hurl plaice.
The moth meant other things and had no equivalent.
The taut lounger sodden with punctured shade.
With the distance fucked out of one another, they
returned from the coffin to The frame, splashed,
took on the colour of Their heads returned to
their heads. But he finished himself off every time
he sat down to One more equivalent: where I came

# Self-Rated AAA

Laika spoke for absent air
        The moon speaks for NASA
Weialala leia spoke for Nature
        $CO_2$ speaks for Prada
Victoria spoke for Empire
        Malala speaks for Birmingham
Dada spoke for Tzara
        The tiara speaks for Dada

# The Price of Nuts

The stage is filled with a billion children,
who run about, blow their whistles, jump and hop,
are naughty, and interfere with the dancing of their superiors.

Vibrant showers of rainbow herbicide scatter the children
and melt the troubling forest, making way
for delegations from significant trading nations

to run about, blow their whistles, hand out samples
and present their slides. I begin to spread out,
taking every available seat and making a scene

in the fog with my laser pointer. Three million
from Andalucía wave Toblerone, their favourite,
and spray warm milk from a repurposed fibre-optic.

Iranian teachers do a do-si-do with cappuccino. More
beautiful than any weather, their caffeinated leaps
correct the Earth's tilt. Pessimism throws up its tiny paws

and submits to the freshly roasted Yirgachefe beans, which
hammer its brain like rain. Guangdong entrepreneurs test
ways to arrive. Their madrigal repeats one hundred times a second,

shuddering the present, as though frustrating a grief.
Each tea-picker takes her turn at offering a leaf of Oolong
to the fearsome and lonely god-bear of Kamchatka.

Summer has turned to autumn and autumn to winter
and the waltz has ended. The bear is flown to New Mexico
where it is buried at Gasbuggy, deep down in the moist

hollow quilted with irritating dreams of uranium-235.
The children return, stouter and more determined to succeed.
Their whistles are broken. They march in groups. The long-haired

have declared the short-haired to have been, all along, their enemy.

# Arguments for a Wall

Across the room their parents do
it. The one listening
doesn't want children at all ever.
Two brothers and a baby sister
sleep through.
The other family
behind the curtain: can't be sure
who each noise belongs to.

The new wall makes it
sexy to do
it in front of people.
Even if the wall
is inside
it you still have to listen
to your parents anyway.
Were your parents your parents though?

Back in the day?
Be honest about
how many children you don't want.
It matters who is bringing
who home even though
my place and your place
are the same place.
Slippery slope to doing yourself.

The wall calls attention
to the chink
by the night or by the hour

through which
you feel wrong as in wrong.
When you're the parents
the room moves around
with your permission

or slowly.
Who were the first
to get a room
and what did they do there?
That fly, what did it see?
Each touches the space
in her own way
or the way they say is right.

Behind the curtain
it sounds like more fun.
The way they sleep,
the way they touch the floor.
Why wouldn't she tidy it up
before she put it in the gallery,
at least make up the bed?
She let herself down.

Someone enters,
checks over the space.
That's nice.
I enter, finally,
as if telling you something,
play the character 'Wall'

to divide the space
into smaller rooms, each a rental.

Each rental is sublet: subtle.
No one has space to do
it. When they do
it, parents cry out
to their children
with pleasure.
Everyone draws
the curtain.

# Today

I storm the parliament building. I force
the illegitimate protestors from
the door of the parliament building. A
faint bruise on my little finger turns out
to have been black rubber from the handle
of my badminton racquet. The pain washes
right off and I find myself nodding
kindly to strangers. My heart stops on the
lumpy B-road following the St Teath
carnival. As the tide comes in on the
Norfolk coast I wade out to the toddler
hooked on the black rocks. I am wrapped in my
bedsheets and taken to a hospital
where agents of the state serve me poison.
I am not going to play football in Chi-
na. I laugh at my friend's little finger
cocked as though drinking tea with the queen un-
til the grenade explodes. Until I ex-
pired in California I was Min-
nie Mouse. For mistaking myself a vic-
tim of a Westminster VIP pae-
dophile ring I enter my cell. On my
smallest knuckle there is a milky scar
recently grown legs and wings. I am tear-
ful as my stunt double breaks my back. My
daughter falls from a cruise ship window. The
hairs on my little finger are unstopp-
able. I will not face a rape charge in
Las Vegas. In my experience it's
the only part of the body complete-

ly useless for sex. I am lined up on
the galley floor by the Iranian
crew. I line up the British crew on the
galley floor of my ship. I feel anxious
suddenly that my little finger is
glossier than the little fingers of
the friends who demand most respect. Is there
a correlation between those with smart
little fingers and those who are rewar-
ded with status and wealth? Since when do I
dislike little fingers based on their rel-
ative glossiness? Since now. Since I mis-
laid my life on the way home from the fu-
neral. Since I spilled into the sea in
a remote and pristine region of Pat-
agonia. Since I dispersed forty
thousand litres of diesel across my
churning surface. Since I swelled through the Pal-
ace gardens holding the rainbow flag. Since
I sprayed bullets at a garlic festi-
val. Since the smell lingered on my little

# Admin

This will end with those lines Keats wrote about his hand expiring that Daisy messaged me with thinking about a poem I might write or something else. I don't know exactly what she was thinking but it worked. Before that I have to turn the device was already on so now it's off. Proprietary waking sound evercla←ear Microsoft Word loading Other device 174808 32 [R] your turn Your Sainsburys.co.uk delivery will arrive today between 16:00–17:00 Authenticating your device Good morning Caleb £28.93 Available: £872.38 I'm thinking the same thing: how am I going to get back to Keats? 'And how do you know what the migrants are thinking?' is what I should have said to the student in the Master's seminar on Tuesday evening Phone Jo K Poem—look @ D redo Alyona Timetable—Helen Click to That warm confusing night I broke into a car by mistake, as some sort of sketch or template for the action about to unfold, I prepare myself to welcome images of other people crashing through this 9:00am clock glance block of text, each with a monologue concerning how I am a beneficiary of their hidden labour. I'm so bored of reviewing this meal, I shout at the hungry waiter, etc. Those dates after the end of the semester for the meeting thing but it is peculiar actually tuning in to the admin, which is like tuning in to static or to tonelessness, somehow the attention and the object cancel each other out. I keep waiting for my admin to look back at me and see a beauty like no beauty it has ever seen; at the ghost in the machine. Satisfied with that line I moved to thumb a device but instead simply thought about thumbing a device and that served almost the same purpose. The difference was in the degree of disappointment. Pressing no screen, I fell roughly a semitone, not off the scale. Often the very sight of my devices excites my insides to an untouchable heat thermometer? as when I am placed in the microwave with the Wheat Bags Original Rectangle Heat Pack &

Ice Pack £9.95 Aroma No thanks Removable cover No thanks Click
to Personalise for £2.50 always wanted one of those and now I
have one of those but only in words. ASPRETTO A CUP FULL
OF POSSIBILITIES which is actually full of mountain green tea,
since it is now afternoon and the music is keeping me on task, the
task in the case of this poem being to stray off task, consciously,
since Daisy and Keats have reminded me of my own mortality and
I have chosen, in response, to record what reminds me that I have
not filled out the spreadsheet with my 'research leave' I promised,
after Liesl asked Richard for special dispensation for me to skip
graduation, I would fill in. Should I do that now? Can I leave you
running while I pop to the server, to access which I will have to
To reset your password please follow this link: BBC Uber Sodexo
Submittable Apple ID Waitrose Bulb Textual Practice Deliveroo
GoDaddy AirBnb Other > Activity Monitor > Sampling process
369 for 3 seconds with 1 millisecond of run time between samples
Sampling completed, processing symbols… Actually borrrrd Did
it, anyway (the spreadsheet) / returned to the section of the library
with the scores TELEMANN BRAHMS SOLOS FOR THE HORN
PLAYER which must be the music I was referring to, as Daisy is
on Spotify and my headphones are piping in the sounds my ears
make. We are now when I have phoned Jo K and spoken to Helen
about the thing with my timetable. But I still don't know what to do
about Alyona's Google Doc—the story of stories—which the Doc
says I haven't accessed for 174808 Are these anyone's keys?
Turned up here via dave … I observe how I might feel if I had
the time: poignant: Dave holding onto his way into my house.
The parcel of blankness which follows might well be the
precise shape and size of the significance of the image, I don't
know. When the whole building shakes, I am here But now

there has been a jump and I have been outside for some time and
returned inside. What had happened was that I have been doing
some searching and it looks like National are still cheapest
 a van drove off the Google Maps B1363 Coconut Lagoon Indian
· ££ into the library. I saw the rump of it (the van) from real-above
and then, as though the van had pierced a big bag holding water,
the water (people) flowed out in a great torrent, but not out of the
hole made by the van but by the sight of the van. When I go outside
everyone is saying, Where is the driver? Where has the driver gone?
and saying so because the drama is structurally unsound with no
human person at its centre. We have finally fought our way to the
deepest heart of the sacred palace, only to find the throne occupied
by Ping: You have two items scheduled for 15:00 Clearly I do
like work. At least twice as much as is Outside I phoned Jo K,
mentioned the van but also tried not to make a fuss and instead
went on about the trouble with my timetable and clashing items
and then there was a commotion and so I couldn't help but narrate
to Jo K what I thought I could see happening, which was flesh
slapping heavily on the wide pavement I feel sick Have you
registered with a new doctor? Not that sort of sick, more like
thinking about Lindsay Lohan, but that reference so the link
Hey everyone, I just want to show you a family that I met they are
Syrian immigrants skip I won't leave until I take you now I
know who you are don't worry you're ruining Arab culture by
doing this I can't believe what just happened even though, in the
last two hours, the connection between Lohan and the van has not
even though, when the two police arrived, they dug out from under
the weight of the concerned citizen who had felled him as he stumb-
led dazed from the scene, a child Scroll back to the beginning of
the poem This will end and ach, I cannot find the reason the child

was driving the vehicle at the beginning of the poem. The soap dispenser is dribbling, should I tell someone? I went to the loo. All that brown feeling flying through the U-bend How many Lindsay Lohans were in the minds of fellow library-goers outside as we heard, we all heard the handsome old policeman's ear cocked like a cat a thud, a scratch and a word(?) come from inside the van. The child driver's face alive with the fear which looks like defiance but crying now. The large citizen vigilante a member of a self-appointed group of citizens who undertake law enforcement in their community basically licked his lips at the sound of the human sound from the van. The handsome old policeman weighs up the risks of getting too close to the van from which black smoke is filling the café but the thud, the scratch and The cat's dead | that'll teach her to be so bold, I have no memory of writing of the pet now a password and decides theatrically to remove his hat, first cue, then strides to the lock on the back of the van and waggles it about Jo K has put on her yellow coat and walked to Highbury Park where she will stand behind a stall selling cakes to raise money for Refugee Action Birmingham A pale Pre-Raphaelite librarian pushes through the crowd bearing an axe. Old handsome policeman takes the axe and looks at it with a passionate intensity. His next movement I describe, even then, as exquisite: an arcing spray of water behind a boat, his arm, extended by the silver axe, looping over his head and down on the lock. What happened next happened a year ago, because Every time I have recounted this story, including in a job interview, I have failed to reach the climactic reveal of what is inside the van, instead skipping to the child's collapse and the medic's screams to Give us some room! Some room! and us drifting frowning to our lonely desks, where we do not see his heart beat or not, from the impact of the crash, or the citizen vigilante's 'arrest', or from seeing, with the rest of us, what flew out of the van, which was

a scarlet macaw has a soul, a language, and a family life modelled on
the pattern of a human (Amerindian) village headed straight for
the top of the tallest tree [look up species]. Mail Three days ago
they said Inside the van? Boxes and boxes of Christmas gloves for
This living hand, now warm and capable / Of earnest grasping [which]
would, if it were cold / And in the icy silence of the tomb, / So haunt
thy days and chill thy dreaming nights / That thou would wish thine own
heart dry of blood / So in my veins red life might stream again, / And
thou be conscience-calm'd—see here it is—/ I hold it towards you.

# The caged lion asks what being a father is like

1. *The morning after your son's birth, all the other animals will gather under a large rock. A mandrill will hold up your son and all the other animals will kneel and celebrate.*

Tying small feet into shoes I need to push the feeling
into every corner of the home. It trips on my behalf
and I find the ladder for the switch. Responsibility
will / began as the teeming water brought
feeling up to the ducts. Wat Tyler, peasant leader,
was covered in human skin. It was sliced through

after he drank in a disgusting fashion before the king's face.

I wish you had put that on our behalf, like the scalpel
entered the numbers into the open-access database.
In my future success there are too many stars
holding the ceiling together. Ants chew the film,
adapting the piece for the present. Otherwise the bread will starve.
If I couldn't speak I would write the word with a knife.

2.   *You will educate your son about the circle of life.*
     *But your brother will excite your son about a dangerous*
     *elephant graveyard. Your son will take his friend to see*
     *the forbidden place.*

As though the official information was still wild.
Trees keep the human from the inner squirrel.
Protection from what? As an adult, you just want
your children to be issued their rightful fake ID.
The satellites delay a world complete with inmates.

Birth gets in on the joke. They look like they are watching TV.
Death, where air, earth and water pile up,
is the Icelandic exclusive fishery zone. One must reveal oneself

To shriek that shriek you'll have to use my mouth
as someone who just is. A baby opens strangers up.
A man with two fathers, I cry double and am half
what a baby needs. I don't want to share pumice,
I don't want to choose wine, but love is practically wild.

3. *You will save your child and his friend from three hyenas in the elephant graveyard. While the hyenas dance and sing with your sinister brother, you will point out dead lions who live in the sky at night and who look like stars.*

A crack in the vocabulary forceps a common
warmth through the North seized the sole.
Strangers hang their own flesh on the frightening stats.
Mourn like plastic bags. A group of animals

colonised a furry yellow membrane to become
your nervous system. One by one the words
like germs. I took off my shoes
so the earth could infect my vote.
How big do you want to be?

Big as someone who can eat himself
My dream to feed myself. A betrayal
to drink water that supported Icelandic ships. No eloquent brick
Can't speak on my daughter's behalf

4.   *Tricked by your bother, you will be trampled to death*
     *by stampeding wildebeest. Your son will believe himself*
     *responsible and run away. Hyenas will move in and*
     *there will be drought.*

because I speak with a different mouf. A daily dab
from the Tester pot of anti-wrinkle serum lets her
see me. Ants witness aliens mowing circles

and shriek. We are used to a certain proportion.
In the Trinity mushroom cloud the face
The pistachio speaks on behalf of Rafsanjan.
The mouth speaks on behalf of the other mithe.
The shipping container contains every other container.
of Joseph, step-father to God's son and to God.
Moth stuck in the foam from the caravan shower.

Outside the warm joke slips down the clown.
When my stomach aches I limp. Road-signs deflect
attention, delaying my parents and their unconditional love.

5.	*Your fatherless son will make friends with a warthog
	and a meerkat. He will grow up living a carefree life
	saying the motto 'hakuna matata' often with the
	wastrels singing and dancing.*

Why fatherhood is like travel: it sends you home.
The crime was to steal the scene: there's no record

of motherhood. The pool has aged to include me
inside it, stared at by a very young girl.
My youth piles up inside her ears, in waves
and waves of judgement. The vocal chords play
the child, hand-crafted in unpleasant resonance
between competing beats. The airport tannoy declares
all passengers have a mouse and a lion inside.
Moths tread softly on your foamy dreams.
We were young, so very young, say your elders.

Why fatherhood is like travel: it sends you home.
The crime was to steal the scene: there's no record

6.   *Your son will be reunited with his friend and will fight your brother to the death. With his enemies gone, your son will take over and it will rain again. The mandrill will present your grandson to the assembled animals, continuing the circle of life.*

of you stepping into those shoes. The centre becomes

the periphery. At the zoo my dog won't look at me.
You're the proper form for the disarray you come from.
The Universe speaks on behalf of Stephen. Old
friends with new themes. She does not feel the love
tonight. What signs are growing inside? Gather books
on flies, flies on the loo books. Class means
I am something I have to transmit.
The eye does not see itself as a habitat. I scrape
the pan with my tiny fingernails. My oval shell
resists plucked heat. Then I run screaming into my daughter's arms.

Here's how to write a letter to your local animal rights organisation.

# Sequel

there comes a time
the time is now
when the characters in the old books
walk out of there
for example
the panther
I saw eating a chicken shamelessly
in a cage
replaced the dead hunger artist
is now in Florida in America
not on holiday sadly
let's call the panther Francis
indigenous to DDT
field → fish → raccoon → Francis can't breed
in a food coma
injected by a scientist with ketamine
placed an electrode in its anus
forcing Francis to come
symbol of freedom
we held hands during take-off
watched the locusts disintegrate
sang the victory song
can we have our symbol back?
tongue flopped on the sanitised table
like a meat
sweet breath of the dealer with the two pairs of trousers
Francis mooches around the swamp
sticky
on my shield
mouse pad
domestic alarm system
inside the bliss

# IKT-SVO

The sun rolls into the chest of the vending machine. Dusk
    tumbles off the shelf.
Four billion chickens close their eyes and dream of dreaming.
    Tucked under

the advancing shade, bodies lie down, row upon row, sinking
    deep into the mosses
growing in the corners of the server. Everywhere the earthworms
    return once again

to their volume on the afterlife. Notions of proximity and
    distance, above and below,
in front and behind, cease to be altogether precise. A cosmonaut,
    whom Gorbachev

had sent up to Mir, still a Soviet citizen, falls in Kazakhstan *as if
    to a foreign land.*
Perched in the nest that hangs from my father's chin, I look
    down at a small child

with no shadows to speak of on my entire body and I laugh. The
    door swings open
and the shopping arrives. The household insects chuckle in the
    less obvious machinery.

Then it became apparent that it was not because we were
    laughing that the house
was falling down. There was a hurricane. A swollen purple face
    bubbled up from the

broadband. Here comes the sun. Only five billion years to wait
    now. I find
myself tumbling out of the sky. I meet my reflection with a
    gentle splash.

As it lumbers over the horizon, plants send their roots deep in
    search of nutrients,
cracking rocks. Domestic canines hear the gentle grinding noise
    as the darkness

is shelved and the people rise, struck by the will to stand.
    The plane lands the same
time it departed. Four billion chickens open their eyes and
    dream of dreaming.

# Prisoner's Dilemma

There's a somewhat technical move unfolding
where the Norwegian Sea meets the Barents Sea.
The purple dust on the Colombian road network
is a pre-emptive strike against the Southern tides,
in phenomenal form. The red plane on Mont Belgica,
pinned by a savage headwind, is already there.
Malaysia has introduced conscription, worth one.
In opposition, rather elegantly, is a large pile
of spent shells on the Nallathanniya NPS Sub Office
employed as a sort of ramp. In terms of Tibet,
a new communications javelin, worth hearing
from, is advancing nicely towards Nam Co.
There is a story about a horse born in that lake.
Pioneering the long-form, gradual approach,
the Sea of Okhostk is walking on its knees.
Some debate about the science is holding back
Arkansas there, and the new turf on the border
messes with points, given the modern walk.
We have sympathy for the Security Council.
When it was my way up through the ranks
it was enough to look up, down, left, right.
In the box here South Africa is down there.
Not one of the best days in terms of deaths.
We want a hurricane with a name please,
west-north-west over clapboard dwellings,
same direction—nice!—as these armed snorkellers
in the Caspian. Smell the love of the Virgin Mary
in Arunachal Pradesh! You'll wait a long time
for a more resounding draw. The yellow busses
are tooling up, and who can blame them, as they

make their southern migration. Puddle farmers,
blights, by themselves with six billion others.
The new nature writing is worth three-fifths,
roughly the rubble in Aleppo. Prime nations
such as Guam really do blow our minds up here.
The sheer weight of insects and insect diaries
is coming up right behind false incarceration.
There are eighty-six golden crowns. Heads
change. Lovely ripple there from a pipe bomb.
Finland can be more than happy with its smog.
That threesome, Norway, Sweden and Finland,
has long looked to scale down. We're seeing
this done in all manner of aggressive ways,
and ten can be multiplied if certain offensive
demographic changes are stoutly defended.
No person, remember, is worth anything.
The Bengal tiger is airborne to keep it angry.
A rather spiky new snow from Naypyitaw
has made an exceptional disturbance in a raft
of memories to do with safety, intrusion, death,
a blunt but effective mode of attack that
(and this is another of the high triumphs of
the Inuit putsch) poisons the broken water.
The Northern Lights are worth five, if time
and foot stamped. We're seeing an overflow
of undergrounds. Chile's employing a typical
defence, tagging the birds to stimulate plastic
production. The replay will clear the rubbish.
The ships, of course, now dominate metal:
firing missiles at the grimacing sunrise,

worth an eastward expansion of tinnitus.
Brno's last crater vies for dominance over
Zlin's hotels. We don't much like to see such
short distances. This baby in Delta Dunării
with three brains will have to be numbered
by committee. This is important because
the beauty of to and fro, attack and defence,
inevitable progress, is in my opinion and
your opinion dependent on the possibility
of revenge. I love this scoreless acid rain in Bol.
We can go to something winning somewhere.
The triumph of Spanish? Brazilian murdered
by hairdresser? The Somali civil service strike
could not be more real. Men dressed in huge
numbers from left to right and from down to up.
I tell you it's a privilege to be alive to see this.
How to come down here from that? Small leaves
fall in Canberra, crudely by their high standards.
Palau-Timor will be gearing up another wind.

# Satire

Joy.

I begin my new employment as Weeds Officer. I conduct extensive surveys of the key breeding grounds across the city. My first task is to secure and defend these strongholds.


A satisfying day.

At sunrise I begin my assault on the tarmac of the city, chief enemy of the weeds. Although by mid-morning I am somewhat disillusioned by the sheer quantity of the material—it is everywhere!—to my relief I discover a yellow vehicle with toothed arms for breaking up tarmac. I am grateful to whomever left this out for my purpose.

By sunset I have made significant progress in establishing deep cracks for water and light to penetrate.


On the move.

My fellow Weeds Officer informs me that the role entails the destruction, rather than the encouragement, of our friends. It seems that my employers interpret the role in the same fashion.

This is true also of the Homeless Officer, whose job I discover involves removing, rather than assisting, the homeless of the city.

But where are they removed to? Is it to the same place that I must be heading?


Flight.

Having learned that it costs less than it would to board the train from my house to the next village, I have purchased an airline ticket. I intend to spend the next few days walking to the airport.


Confusion.

I recite my data:
O-
EVERCLEAR
24.11.1983

KINGS HEATH PRIMARY
ADMIN@FRIENDLYWEED.NET
1H 11M PER DAY ^34% FROM LAST WEEK

I stand beaming, if slightly out of breath, in front of my interlocutor. The man looks at me as though I am his house plant.

'Passport?' he asks.

Hope.

On our descent there is an announcement that the air to which we have all contributed is available to purchase. It is a unique souvenir, says the weary announcement, of the time we have spent together this afternoon.

I have enjoyed the company and smell of these strangers, conversation with whom I imagine would be delightful, and am moved to buy several bottles of our air, including a slightly more expensive limited edition which comes with a vial of our dust.

Happy memories.

Today in a restaurant I am served a mound of vegetables which I had, only a few weeks ago, thrown away. On them the taste of myself is unmistakeable. Not only that but my companion, with whom I share the meal, instantly asks me in sympathy about the pain in my little finger, a pain which I have kept entirely private and indeed I can barely muster the courage to speak of it to myself, and yet the vegetables have informed my companion.

A setback.

I have learned that beef burgers are cows in another, dead form and that milk is a liquid produced by cows to feed their own young, who are forcibly removed from their mothers in order for the nourishment to bypass them, bottled for me instead.

Pleasurable failure.

My attempt to suckle a calf has ended in failure. After an initial, robust interest in my tender, salty areola, the calf removes its tongue to some other, more familiar quarter of the field. The sensation of the calf's tongue on my skin is almost unbearably pleasurable.

Once again on the move.


Love.

I am about to clean the brown streaks from the handrail on the stairs in the flat where I am lodging when I pause to ask the handrail how it would like to be remembered.

'Common cold, urine, salt, pollen, chlorine,' it says. 'But above all, to have been loved.'


Disappearance.

This afternoon a couple arrive at the flat. They open the door and walk in as though they own the place. When I speak, they appear not to hear me. When they remove my desk and bring in a large dining table, they and their table pass through me.

As I leave, the new cat bites my invisible heel. The cat bleeds.

# explanatory notes
# with no fingers

2 I started in writing what would become this collection in 2013 and and I just published the first collection interpret angry and upset about that embarrassed about what I done but didn't understand why

why the City with an ancient wall right round it and Roman earrings I was Janet which took a ear to write started off and some love sonnets became much more compressed and

and I was writing myself out of a hole I thought that actually was writing myself into a hole I think and Other Poems came as I was writing to a joyful bigger and bigger and

bigger inflating when a TN or Star is dying it gets bigger in bigger and that's how you know it's nearly expired it comes colossal how much writing was found to be on the right size

size of what passes through me when my send my voice out what comes back what happens to other people's voices inside me what kind of sieve I am

to my wife who is also the writer and I'm the cut to her and I I want her to like one too and I had this idea you know when you tell someone my dear you say hey Adam miss little thing and it's going to be about global injustice

funny because you hear something else come back and she is such a brilliant idea to what my little finger thinks about me and of course that's much better idea than the idea that I thought I've been telling

and all the time are plastic lodged in your stomach which is called Xanax in Sligo and all of these comments 2 to come back to me as feedback like if something cutting across the medium I can speed boat

or your brother asked you to write him a Wikipedia page then you write Wikipedia page then the Wikipedia people say that your Wikipedia page on your brother is not properly what kind of evidence you might be able to

about this man who surely you no as well as the haha or around body to man who plays gym when you're a child in those pieces of plastic that have come through from tubes in the back was my favourite

circulating water around Bath making waterfalls driving turbines that was always my favourite thing anyway memories of my brothers because I'm really not playing with me

in the bath and so Will be a kind of silt of me in this that I have seduced so they will be kind to me when I say audio in Audible dusted off big are his sorrow enormous

just incredibly moving is videos of people watching grass eating lunch the kind of thing you watch when you're asleep and the people who are in the videos would never ever know and their dogs

coming back to your self called plastic that you are alive is built from distant literary but you can't visualise that misery and so so you just feel that your life should itself be more miserable

like a late winter Sky watching Gardeners World with your mum and the most pleasant thing in their little thing child couldn't be happier so that becomes the poem

and and there's feel that you're driving around at night and you want to lose the thread somehow so that it becomes cotton again it goes back to the plant it unravels at to the prickly plant in the song

crying and crying at Mufasa and and the ticks that live on Mufasa and birds that live on the ticks on dead so everyone is dead and it's like scrolling back and you have words instead of fingers or fingers at the tips of my words feeling The Shining plane rubbing hot fuselage of the pain which will take you over the x x x and x as well

Kind of thinking well now we can travel the speed now that we can can Fly now that we can look down from there can we meet shadow in the same way

When NASA Nike NASA and the dark Russian dog would have eaten how many Russian cows and is it stomach in space cremated on entry

their little thing the ants in the wind watching peregrines nesting on kids in North Wales and in the couldn't be happier

my dear my dear my dear you say hey I didn't miss little thing and it's going to be back open and justice you can hear the chattel downstairs

thank you about the gas money going out steam condensation on the walls

it's a list tuple of lists just like a to-do list the people to do this

# Love in reverse
# is evolution

Space spins around the globe. The clay moulds the fingers and the fingers soil the clay. The soiled fingers are made of carbon and oxygen, hydrogen, nitrogen, calcium. Skin cells are siloed from the host. The mountain climbs slowly below the mountaineer's slick hands. The rock cups the clinging fingertips and liquid flows up the cliff. The mountain is a pile of bodies. The mystery inside the stone is a silt of sea creatures. The cliff remembers the Archean Eon. The sea creatures teach the mountaineer to breathe. The oxygen asks the lips to say *O*. The oxygen canister also contains life. The alveolus cell expels imprisoned air. The rain collects carbon dioxide. The local granite sifts the alien rain. The cycle allocates the precious waste. The kaolin gathers oxygen and hydrogen, aluminium and silicon. The clay globe cools the kiln.

One stratum of clay slips under the continental plate. A rope of bubbles descends from the upper thermocline. The swimmer reaches the sea bed. Oxygen rises with desire. It takes years for the inside of the oyster to become nacreous. It takes eons for the strata to concertina. The waves are moved by fronds of kelp. The submarine pilot is on dry land. The oxygen and hydrogen remove themselves. The sodium and the chlorine remain. The saline residue forms crystals on the skin, under the rock and inside the clam. Sprayed glaze hardens the tiles against reactive oxygen. The seashell's lips are crusted over with salt. The clam hosts a million living beings. It is snug inside the wetsuit. The closed shell keeps in the sea.

Beaks open. Dawn sings to the birds. Cool water calls time on the night. Worms rise to catch the birds' attention. Wings carry dust that seeds a drop of rain. The drop is drawn down to the ocean. Light warms the surface. The upper thermocline is tense with life. The drifting plant cracks open a wasted breath. The human eye requires curved glass to see the tiny creature. From space the room becomes a petri dish. The creature peering down the microscope becomes its microscopic guest. The body holds the skeleton in place. Internal organs create vapour. The vapour remembers to drift. Each chink becomes an open window.

The air resists the glass. Particles invite the nose to see the early planet. Aeons concertina. The nose hears how the earth was molten red. Sea shuts around the earth and tamps the flames. Leaves and wood amend volcanic land. Rich animal musk becomes a map. Desire lines the air. Pollen seeks a mate and finds a nose. The territory eddies and swirls. The internal combustion engine invents the modern road. Microbes fly by soot. Drifting plants graze on warming carbon. Ancient photosynthesis makes oceans slick with life. Clouds chew air and spit. The mouth takes nitrogen to make the muscles, blink the eye and turn the nose. Light trapped in cells of ocean life rains down towards the floor. The body, rich in nutrients, becomes bright coral. Space moves through its branches.

world around the

The eye does not see itself as a place to live.
The cruise ship parties on a bellyful of jellyfish.

Painted stars hold the cracked ceiling together.
Light falls and the sea is supportive.

My debt shoves me aside and grins at the camera.
When a number forgets where it started, it speculates.

Coins multiply in the frozen hearts of Bluefin tuna.
This coin will forever bear another's head.

# The sun looks in
# and the whole world with it

I remember the first portrait with an open window
and through the window, a landscape, and in the
landscape, other people, and each of these people
should have their own portrait by an open window

but as far as I know they do not. The landscape
perched on the sitter's shoulder like a tame parrot
feathered with peasants: a bird trained to sense
the kind of silence that invites, like an open window,

a presence to fill the empty frame, which in this
case is a squawked *Hello*, a greeting that, to our
relief, will not blossom into pleasantries, saving us
the awkwardness of leaning through the open window

to ask *And what do you do?* because all the parrot
made of peasants *does* is it says *Hello*. What *you* do
is look. I remember the portrait was what my eyes
felt like to leave his house, the window closed

behind me. The old man had seasoned his bedroom
with salt, to kill the mites that I could not see
but which looked to him like salt. After sunset
they came, he said, straight through the open window.

# Sunset

I turned the corner and spied a nice shell.
I clamped onto the arm, pulled out the
body and crawled in. I heard the sea
inside. I crawled along the beach. It
was light and the shell was cracked.
I went under a rock. I went under a rock.
I went under a rock. I swapped vehicle
for an empty shell. In the shell the salt
made me feel odd. The dark seaweed
crackled. The air was empty and
confusing. It was as though it was
the wrong instrument. It might have
been another storm. The guy from
before was crawling around a pool.
I crawled away from the dark seaweed.
I crawled around the pool. I was
crawling around the pool but then I
headed for the warm water bubbling
out of the pipe. The horizon in the
warm water was further than I thought.
I crawled for a while. I felt odd with
no crackling. I set down the shell.
The shell's shape is truly excellent.
I found a pair of ants on someone else
so that I could listen to them while I
looked around the warm water. I
crawled along the sand to the edge of
the bubbling water. I crawled around
the bubbling water. I turned in the other
direction. It was the same. But the

original direction was better. I span
in that direction. The sun was going
down. There was a nice shell but I
did not get it. I thought that in the
warm water I would see something else.
There was darkness coming through.
I drew warm sand over my back. The
ants were gone. I threw aside a pebble
and climbed down. The music in the
tunnel was like water dripping on water.
There was so much darkness. I crawled
through the tunnel. I crawled through
the tunnel. I crawled through and then
it was too dark and then I went on.

# Flying Over 'Mont Blanc'

### I

The everlasting universe of things
Flows through the mind, and rolls its rapid waves,
Now dark—now glittering—now reflecting gloom—
Now lending splendour, where from secret springs
The source of human thought its tribute brings
Of waters,—with a sound but half its own,
Such as a feeble brook will oft assume,
In the wild woods, among the mountains lone,
Where waterfalls around it leap for ever,
Where woods and winds contend, and a vast river
Over its rocks ceaselessly bursts and raves.

### II

Thus thou, Ravine of Arve—dark, deep Ravine—
Thou many-colour'd, many-voiced vale,
Over whose pines, and crags, and caverns sail
Fast cloud-shadows and sunbeams: awful scene,
Where Power in likeness of the Arve comes down
From the ice-gulfs that gird his secret throne,
Bursting through these dark mountains like the flame
Of lightning through the tempest;—thou dost lie,
Thy giant brood of pines around thee clinging,
Children of elder time, in whose devotion
The chainless winds still come and ever came
To drink their odours, and their mighty swinging
To hear—an old and solemn harmony;
Thine earthly rainbows stretch'd across the sweep
Of the aethereal waterfall, whose veil
Robes some unsculptur'd image; the strange sleep
Which when the voices of the desert fail
Wraps all in its own deep eternity;
Thy caverns echoing to the Arve's commotion,
A loud, lone sound no other sound can tame;
Thou art pervaded with that ceaseless motion,
Thou art the path of that unresting sound—
Dizzy Ravine! and when I gaze on thee
I seem as in a trance sublime and strange
To muse on my own separate fantasy,
My own, my human mind, which passively
Now renders and receives fast influencings,
Holding an unremitting interchange
With the clear universe of things around;
One legion of wild thoughts, whose wandering wings
Now float above thy darkness, and now rest
Where that or thou art no unbidden guest,
In the still cave of the witch Poesy,
Seeking among the shadows that pass by
Ghosts of all things that are, some shade of thee,
Some phantom, some faint image; till the breast
From which they fled recalls them, thou art there!

### III

Some say that gleams of a remoter world
Visit the soul in sleep, that death is slumber,
And that its shapes the busy thoughts outnumber
Of those who wake and live.—I look on high;
Has some unknown omnipotence unfurl'd
The veil of life and death? or do I lie
In dream, and does the mightier world of sleep
Spread far around and inaccessibly
Its circles? For the very spirit fails,
Driven like a homeless cloud from steep to steep
That vanishes among the viewless gales!
Far, far above, piercing the infinite sky,
Mont Blanc appears—still, snowy, and serene;
Its subject mountains their unearthly forms
Pile around it, ice and rock; broad vales between
Of frozen floods, unfathomable deeps,
Blue as the overhanging heaven, that spread
And wind among the accumulated steeps;
A desert peopled by the storms alone,
Save when the eagle brings some hunter's bone,
And the wolf tracks her there—how hideously
Its shapes are heap'd around! rude, bare, and high,
Ghastly, and scarr'd, and riven.—Is this the scene
Where the old Earthquake-daemon taught her young
Ruin? Were these their toys? or did a sea
Of fire envelop once this silent snow?
None can reply—all seems eternal now.
The wilderness has a mysterious tongue
Which teaches awful doubt, or faith so mild,
So solemn, so serene, that man may be,
But for such faith, with Nature reconcil'd;
Thou hast a voice, great Mountain, to repeal
Large codes of fraud and woe; not understood
By all, but which the wise, and great, and good
Interpret, or make felt, or deeply feel.

### IV

The fields, the lakes, the forests, and the streams,
Ocean, and all the living things that dwell
Within the daedal earth; lightning, and rain,
Earthquake, and fiery flood, and hurricane,
The torpor of the year when feeble dreams
Visit the hidden buds, or dreamless sleep
Holds every future leaf and flower; the bound
With which from that detested trance they leap;
The works and ways of man, their death and birth,
And that of him and all that his may be;
All things that move and breathe with toil and sound
Are born and die; revolve, subside, and swell.
Power dwells apart in its tranquillity,

Remote, serene, and inaccessible:
And this, the naked countenance of earth,
On which I gaze, even these primeval mountains
Teach the adverting mind. The glaciers creep
Like snakes that watch their prey, from their far fountains,
Slow rolling on; there, many a precipice
Frost and the Sun in scorn of mortal power
Have pil'd: dome, pyramid, and pinnacle,
A city of death, distinct with many a tower
And wall impregnable of beaming ice.
Yet not a city, but a flood of ruin
Is there, that from the boundaries of the sky
Rolls its perpetual stream; vast pines are strewing
Its destin'd path, or in the mangled soil
Branchless and shatter'd stand; the rocks, drawn down
From yon remotest waste, have overthrown
The limits of the dead and living world,
Never to be reclaim'd. The dwelling-place
Of insects, beasts, and birds, becomes its spoil;
Their food and their retreat for ever gone,
So much of life and joy is lost. The race
Of man flies far in dread; his work and dwelling
Vanish, like smoke before the tempest's stream,
And their place is not known. Below, vast caves
Shine in the rushing torrents' restless gleam,
Which from those secret chasms in tumult welling
Meet in the vale, and one majestic River,
The breath and blood of distant lands, for ever
Rolls its loud waters to the ocean-waves,
Breathes its swift vapours to the circling air.

### V

Mont Blanc yet gleams on high:—the power is there,
The still and solemn power of many sights,
And many sounds, and much of life and death.
In the calm darkness of the moonless nights,
In the lone glare of day, the snows descend
Upon that Mountain; none beholds them there,
Nor when the flakes burn in the sinking sun,
Or the star-beams dart through them. Winds contend
Silently there, and heap the snow with breath
Rapid and strong, but silently! Its home
The voiceless lightning in these solitudes
Keeps innocently, and like vapour broods
Over the snow. The secret Strength of things
Which governs thought, and to the infinite dome
Of Heaven is as a law, inhabits thee!
And what were thou, and earth, and stars, and sea,
If to the human mind's imaginings
Silence and solitude were vacancy?

*Away From Me* by Caleb Klaces
Published by Prototype in 2021

The right of Caleb Klaces to be identified as author of this work has been asserted in accordance with Section 77 of the UK Copyright, Designs and Patents Act 1988.

Copyright © Caleb Klaces 2021
All rights reserved

No part of this publication may be reproduced, stored in a retrieval system, or transmitted, in any form or by any means, electronic, mechanical, photocopying, recording or otherwise, without the prior permission of the publishers. A CIP record for this book is available from the British Library.

Design by Studio Foss
Typeset in Tiempos Text
Printed in the UK by TJ Books

ISBN 978-1-913513-15-3

( )   (         )    p      prototype

(type 1 – poetry)
www.prototypepublishing.co.uk
@prototypepubs

Prototype Publishing
71 Oriel Road
London E9 5SG
UK

( )